Writing by Doing

3rd Edition
Teacher's Manual

Writing by Doing

Learning to Write Effectively

Elaine Hughes
David A. Sohn

National Textbook Company
a division of *NTC Publishing Group* • Lincolnwood, Illinois USA

Published by National Textbook Company, a division of NTC Publishing Group.
©1997, 1990, 1983 NTC Publishing Group, 4255 West Touhy Avenue,
Lincolnwood (Chicago), Illinois 60646-1975 U.S.A.
All rights reserved. No part of this book may be reproduced, stored
in a retrieval system, or transmitted in any form or by any means,
electronic, mechanical, photocopying, recording or otherwise, without
prior permission of NTC Publishing Group.
Manufactured in the United States of America.

6 7 8 9 VP 0 9 8 7 6 5 4 3 2 1

CONTENTS

About *Writing by Doing*   1
     Audience   1
     Organization   1
     Features   2
     Strategy   2
     Using the Text   3
     A Note on Paragraph Style   4

Some Tips for the Classroom   5
     Incorporating Writing into the Classroom   5
     Using the Portfolio Method   5

PART 1   PERSONAL WRITING: Writing for Yourself   7

Chapter 1   The Journal   9
Chapter 2   Using Your Powers of Observation and Imagination   13
Chapter 3   Your Autobiography   15
Chapter 4   The Personal Letter   17

PART 2   PARAGRAPH POWER: Developing Your Ideas Step by Step   19

Chapter 5   Writing Effective Paragraphs   21
Chapter 6   Descriptive Paragraphs   23
Chapter 7   Narrative Paragraphs   24
Chapter 8   Expository Paragraphs   25
Chapter 9   Persuasive Paragraphs   27

PART 3   LONGER COMPOSITIONS: Writing for Others   29

Chapter 10   Writing an Essay   31

Chapter 11	The Factual Report	33
Chapter 12	The Review	34
Chapter 13	Business Communications	35
PART 4	LANGUAGE SKILLS REVIEW: A Quick Reference for Correct Usage Answer Key	37
Chapter 14	Sentence Sense	39
Chapter 15	Building Sentences with Phrases and Clauses	46
Chapter 16	Verb Power	55
Chapter 17	Troublesome Verbs	59
Chapter 18	Using Correct Pronouns	64
Chapter 19	Subject-Verb Agreement	66
Chapter 20	Words often Misused or Misspelled	69
Chapter 21	Punctuation	73
Chapter 22	Using Apostrophes and Quotations	78
Chapter 23	Capitalization and Abbreviation	82

Selected Bibliography   87

About *Writing by Doing*

AUDIENCE

Now in its third edition, *Writing by Doing* was written to develop the writing skills of a student who can read the text and understand what it says. We assume that the student previously has developed some writing ability, but that he or she can benefit greatly from an organized approach in writing instruction. Even those students already capable of writing well will gain from using this book.

Students functioning at the fourth stanine or better in reading ability on standardized tests such as the California Achievement Test, the Metropolitan Achievement Test, or the Iowa Test of Basic Skills probably can handle the instruction in this book and improve their writing ability. The book can even be used with students who have difficulty reading by reading the instruction aloud to the students and working closely and slowly with them on the exercises and the activities.

This book is developmental in the sense that it can alleviate many of the problems that students have with writing, help them to develop confidence in their writing abilities, and provide them with satisfaction when they see that they can use the process of writing to communicate well with others and to express clearly their own ideas.

ORGANIZATION

Writing by Doing is divided into four main parts:

Part 1 Personal Writing: Writing for Yourself
Part 2 Paragraph Power: Developing Your Ideas Step by Step
Part 3 Longer Compositions: Writing for Others
Part 4 Language Skills Review: A Quick Reference for Correct Usage

The first three parts instruct students in improving the process of writing, beginning with finding pleasure and power through personal writing, moving to developing paragraphs as a manageable method for understanding many of the basics of the composing process, and ending with longer compositions—more formal papers that students are called upon to write for others.

Part 4, the longest part, includes ten chapters and provides students with a means for reviewing and practicing specific skills involving sentence structure, correct usage, and language mechanics. This section is intended to serve as a quick reference that students can use often and easily.

FEATURES

Each of the first three parts begins with an introduction and a brief list entitled "What You Will Learn." In addition, the first 13 chapters include the following features:

- *Warm-up*—introduces each chapter and is designed to motivate students to learn about the skills to be taught and to help them recognize how they are presently applying these skills.
- *Introductory Information*—conveys essential information in concise paragraphs that introduce and expand the chapter topics.
- *Writing Activities*—numerous writing activities that give students hands-on experience with the concept previously presented. Writing Activities are numbered consecutively within each chapter and vary in quantity according to the level of complexity and the amount of time required to complete each activity.

Each chapter of Part 4, "Language Skills Review," conveys pertinent information followed by Skills Activities. The chapters then conclude with one or more Skill Tests. The answer key for both the Skills Activities and the Skill Tests are grouped at the end of this *Teacher's Manual*.

- *Skills Activity*—designed to provide a quick review of a specific skill. This opportunity for practice reinforces the previous information given.
- *Skill Test*—one or more tests that can be used either as a student self-test or as a test to be graded. These tests serve as a cumulative review of all the information presented in the chapter.

Students should be able to work independently with the activities and tests in Part 4. However, we recommend that the teacher supplement specific skills in the classroom with personal instruction. Though not a grammar text, the "Language Skills Review" enables a teacher to review specific skills with his or her class, with small groups, or with individual students. Fostering these skills in depth, however, probably will require the use of a standard grammar text.

STRATEGY

The core of the instruction concerning the process of writing is in Parts 1, 2, and 3. The program instructs students in specific skills, presenting the information in a format that is brief enough not to overwhelm, yet provides adequate information to apply to a writing activity. Because the writing activities are relatively short, they can be easily evaluated by the teacher. As students improve with each assignment and experience regular success, the confidence that success can inspire should have powerful, beneficial effects on students' attitudes toward writing.

The pace of the program can be adjusted according to the teacher's schedule and the students' level of understanding of the material. However, it is not strict adherence to a lesson plan that will ensure student success; rather, their success depends upon being given ample opportunities to learn by writing. By addressing the process of writing on three levels—the academic level, the personal level, and the practical level—students learn to use writing as a tool for school and college, for personal pleasure, and for the business and professional world.

USING THE TEXT

There are several effective ways to use this book. Much depends upon the needs of the students, the instructional style of the teacher, and the limitations of the school setting. Here are three suggested ways to incorporate *Writing by Doing* in your teaching program:

1. *The Linear Approach.* This book has been organized to be used effectively by beginning at the beginning of the book and working through chronologically to the end. It moves from personal writing to paragraph development, the multiparagraph essay, and practical writing for the business world. As the teacher encounters problems with mechanics, sentence structure, or language usage, specific problems can be addressed through the appropriate reviews in Part 4, "Language Skills Review." Instruction can be individualized at the discretion of the teacher.

   Lessons in the "Language Skills Review" can be used for diagnosis as well as review. The teacher can determine whether most of the class needs work in a given skill. If so, the students can work with the grammar text that is normally used with the class to teach the skill in greater depth.

2. *Alternative Organization.* The teacher may wish to teach the sections of the book in another order. For example, the teacher might want to begin instruction with the paragraph and move to the multiparagraph essay. After these sections, personal writing might be introduced, and finally, practical writing.

3. *The Partial Approach.* Some teachers may feel that students need to work with only parts of the book. An advanced class may use sections on paragraph development, the multiparagraph essay, and personal writing, for example. Another group may need to work with much of the "Language Skills Review" in combination with sharpening sentence skills until the class is ready to proceed to more sophisticated writing.

A NOTE ON PARAGRAPH STYLE

As you read *Writing by Doing*, you will notice that most of the paragraphs are not indented. This style of paragraphing is called the "block style." Books and magazines frequently use the block style of paragraphing as part of the design. Many businesses are now employing the block style of paragraphing because it saves time for the typist and looks more stylish to many people.

It has been the tradition in teaching composition, however, to instruct students to indent each paragraph when it is written on paper or typed. According to personal preference, then, the teacher may make the choice between indent and block style. As a general note, however, it may be advisable to explain to students that the block style is employed in many books, magazines, and business letters, while indentation is ordinarily used with handwritten work and much work that is typed.

Some Tips for the Classroom

INCORPORATING WRITING INTO THE CLASSROOM

Often, covering all that students must learn in the traditional high school English class is so overwhelming that many teachers forgo altogether the opportunities for student practice writing. This is unfortunate, because writing is the singular activity that helps students integrate all other English language skills. Indeed, the best way students can learn to write is to require them to write regularly.

However, the traditional approach of the teacher's collecting all written work and reading and marking it for hours on end is certain to rob both teacher and students of the pleasures of writing. One alternative is to decide in advance that you will not read all that students write in the classroom. Instead, you will focus on giving students frequent opportunities to write. Then, as the class progresses, students can be asked to read what they have written aloud to their peers—either in small groups or to the class as a whole. In hearing their own words as they read them aloud, students recognize how they use language and gain a sense of pride in their work, as well. Writing becomes a privilege rather than a chore. A teacher may opt to select a few compositions for closer reading and assessment, without being bound by the old method of being the only person who responds to a student's writing.

Keep in mind that in-class writings do not have to be long. In fact, brief writing periods of 5–10 minutes in which students practice writing rapidly without stopping can be followed, if time permits, by a read-aloud period. If done at the beginning of class meetings, these short writings can serve to involve students the minute the class period begins. Short in-class writing opportunities can be built into the class schedule, say, two or three times a week, so that students come to expect that they will write on given days. Most of the time these writings can become entries in students' journals. Sometimes, however, you may choose to collect a specific assignment to read through quickly and comment upon.

Out-of-class writings may be handled in a like manner, incorporating some of the work into the journal and collecting some for assessment and grading.

USING THE PORTFOLIO METHOD

The portfolio method serves both teacher and students. All that is needed is a file labeled with the name of each student. When papers are due or a particular in-class writing assignment is collected, the file folders are distributed and each student places the assigned paper in his or her personal folder and returns the folder immediately to the teacher. Over time, students gain a sense of pride as they see their quantity of writings increase and the quality of their work improve.

Once the papers are collected in the folders, they are available for reading and assessing at any given time. Seeing the full scope of a student's work helps immeasurably in directing that student. It is much easier to follow a student's progress when using the portfolio method. Grading becomes more holistic when the full range of the student's work is at hand during the evaluation process.

As much as possible, place the responsibility with the student for keeping the portfolio neatly arranged. Insist that the papers be placed, bottom to top, in the order that they were written. In addition, it's a good idea to have students date each paper as well as title it. It's interesting to have students read papers they wrote months previously so that they may gauge their improvement. They may note a pattern of similar writing errors in their work, such as misspelled words, for example. To help students address this pattern, have them use the inside covers of their folders to list troublesome spelling words or errors that they make repeatedly.

For further benefit, at several points throughout the year review the writing portfolio with each student. Also, students can be organized in small groups and use their portfolios for peer evaluation.

Part 1 Personal Writing: Writing for Yourself

GOALS

In Part 1, students will learn how to:

- keep a journal in order to develop confidence as a writer, capture memories, develop a writing voice, and expand writing style.
- use their powers of observation and imagination.
- research, write, and revise an autobiographical sketch.
- write different kinds of personal letters.

Chapter 1   The Journal

This chapter includes the following headings:
- Why Keep a Journal? (p. 3)
- Setting Up Your Journal (p. 4)
- Making a Journal Entry (p. 6)
- Capturing Memories (p. 8)
- Your Writing Voice (p. 9)
- Expanding Your Writing Style (p. 11)

In addition, 15 Writing Activities are placed throughout the chapter.

JOURNAL WRITING

Through the centuries, men and women have kept journals, diaries, and logs. They have kept them for a variety of reasons. Journals can provide a valuable record of day-by-day experiences. Since the human memory is not always reliable or precise, journals can be valuable as an accurate record of the past. Some writers have kept a journal as a problem-solving device. Writing about personal problems may help clarify them and may lead to solutions.

The process of keeping a journal reflects the central idea of this writing program. Daily writing about personal thoughts and impressions offers the student a regular opportunity to learn writing by doing. Such writing can be more meaningful to a student than practice exercises in class. Indeed, encouraging the journal habit at any stage in one's life can be valuable because it may provide a memory book of great pleasure for later years.

Keeping a journal is an activity that should build a writer's confidence. Absence of correction and freedom of expression have beneficial effects upon writing. The more one regularly crystallizes his or her thoughts on paper, the greater one's confidence in the written word can become.

An important technique is introduced at this stage in the text. It employs the familiar set of questions that journalists frequently use—the 5Ws and H. *Then, Now,* and *Someday* are added to these thought-provokers to provide a structure for initiating thoughts to write about.

THE PUBLIC JOURNAL AND THE PRIVATE JOURNAL

Students will be asked to do journal exercises in a classroom setting. Such exercises are part of a public journal. A public journal contains information that may be shared with others in the class, including the teacher, at any time. A private journal, on the other hand, is personal property, under the absolute control of the student. No student should be required to reveal the writings in his or her private journal. All students should clearly understand the difference between the *public journal*, which is to be shared, and the *private journal*, which need not be shared.

Activities

When beginning the process of journal keeping, the following is a good activity to use as a starter:

1. Ask students to keep a public journal, written in class, for one week. The purpose of this is to learn the mechanics of keeping a journal and to experience the pleasure of building a journal.
   a. Go carefully over the 5 Ws and H (plus *Then*, *Now*, and *Someday*) questions. Be certain that these questions lead to thought flow. They can be applied to anything that will promote journal writing. The text presents how the questions work, but some students may misunderstand the purpose of the questions as stimulators. It may be helpful to use the previous hour's experience as an example and model. Apply the questions to what happened to you in the previous hour and show students how these could be used in writing a journal entry.
   b. Each day, devote 10 to 15 minutes to an entry in the public journal. Review the 5Ws and H technique for stimulating journal writing. Allow students to write their entries. After time is called, have several students share their entries with the class. Discuss these entries, but make no evaluative judgments about them. Emphasize the importance of recording detail and of giving the reader a clear picture of the experience. Many students enjoy this activity. Point out that details that may seem trivial now could turn out to be important later.
   c. The week's public journal kept in class is preparation for the private journal. Students now are to keep a daily journal. This journal will be private. The only requirement will be to demonstrate to the teacher that entries are being made in it daily.
2. Read excerpts from diaries and journals that have been kept by both famous and ordinary people. If you have a well-stocked public library, you should be able to find ample examples under the diary or journal sections. *Anne Frank: The Diary of a Young Girl* is an excellent model for students. Other people who kept jour-

nals that have been published are Thomas Edison, Christopher Columbus, Amelia Earhart, Davy Crockett, Dag Hammarskjold, Theodore Roosevelt, and Queen Victoria. Reading examples aloud to the students will demonstrate to them how the journal can give the reader a feeling for the past as filtered through the eyes and the mind of the writer.

3. Sometimes students have trouble starting a journal entry. Suggest that they read the newspaper, select one or two stories, and react to the stories in the journal. For instance, a student might support or object to an opinion expressed in an editorial.
4. Another good starter for a journal is to discuss a television program or a movie in the journal. Writing about the strong and weak points of the experience is excellent practice in writing.
5. If you wish to assign a public journal for another week, have each student write a journal entry about what happened in your class the day before. Discuss the entries after they are written. This activity will provide valuable practice for the students and will also offer interesting insights for you concerning how your students view your classroom activities.

YOUR WRITING VOICE

Keeping a journal is an excellent way to work toward developing a good "writing voice." We do not write exactly as we speak. The writing should sound natural, but the naturalness should not be forced. A good writing voice reflects the personality of the writer and is very much a part of a writer's style.

Unlike everyday speech, the writer composes in complete sentences most of the time. Written language should have rhythm and appeal, but it should also have clarity and organization. The reader should be able to "hear" the writer.

All journal entries encourage a personal focus. Encourage students to read each entry aloud. This practice will help them discover what sounds natural and what sounds too formal or stilted. It will also help students detect errors and omissions.

To further increase a student's awareness of his or her writing voice, suggest using a tape recorder. If possible, all students should be given opportunities to read their journal selections into a tape recorder and listen to the playback.

Activities

1. Read the journal entries for a week into a tape recorder. Listen to them carefully. Then write a summary of the week's experience.
2. Group students in pairs. Have the partners exchange their public journals. Each partner should read the other's journal aloud. This activity will give each writer

a different perspective on his or her work. It should also be a measure of the ease with which the selection can be read.
3. Have students read the journals or autobiographies of famous people aloud to the class. Point out the individual voices that emerge from these journal entries. This exercise is an excellent way to demonstrate what "writing voice" means.

Chapter 2   Using Your Powers of Observation and Imagination

This chapter includes the following headings:
- Using Your Powers of Observation (p. 22)
- Using Your Powers of Imagination (p. 33)

In addition, 18 writing activities are placed throughout the chapter.

The activities in this chapter are designed to help students strengthen their ability to observe and imagine. Close observations will lead to more vivid student writing. Students will focus on specific details, especially details that appeal to the five senses. Encouraging writers to expand their imaginative powers and to use their "inner eye" will give them confidence that they can always find material to write about—simply by tapping their own imaginations.

Observation Activities

1. An enjoyable and valuable activity for improving observation is to have each student bring to class a small object. Collect the objects and redistribute them so that a student gets a different object from the one he or she brought in. After a period of close observation, say five minutes, choose a student to stand and describe the object he or she was handed without showing it. The rest of the class will use the description given to guess the object. Afterward, the object can be revealed and the class can decide how accurate the student's description of the object was and what might have been added or omitted.

2. Since using our powers of observation is always centered in the awareness of our five senses, you might want to emphasize how important it is to develop this awareness. A very quick and simple exercise for increasing the powers of the five senses is a "Here-and-Now" activity. Ask students to be very quiet for a few minutes so that they may become aware of each of their five senses. Instruct them to write three sentences on each of the five senses, for a total of 15 sentences. Each of the sentences can begin "Right now I see . . . ," "Right now I smell . . . ," and so forth. Encourage students to use some of the methods learned in Chapter 1 for increasing vividness of language, such as incorporating similes and metaphors into their written descriptions.

Imagination Activities

Urge students to reacquaint themselves with their innate imaginations, especially if they feel (as many students do) that they have lost their ability to imagine. Emphasize the value of a rich and active imagination for a writer. Invite students to go back to childhood dreams, daydreams, and fantasies, revisiting their natural tendency to imagine. Most students can easily remember how vivid their imaginations used to be in early childhood.

1. Ask students to make a detailed list of some dreams, fantasies, or ideas they remember having as young children. Have them expand the one that still is intriguing, developing their early imaginings into a fully written journal entry or short paper. Emphasize that an imaginative child still lives within each one of us, offering a resource for every writer.

2. Encourage students to develop their inner eye by closing their eyes and imagining a giant TV screen onto which they can project the imaginings of their minds, as if the action of a movie was developing right in front of them. In the classroom, have students sit up straight and close their eyes. Begin by asking the class to project an article of clothing—such as a sweater—onto their personal screens and then direct the class to change the color of the sweater several times. Later, as the class progresses in ability, name four or five objects or people to be projected onto each student's screen to come to life in a scene. For example, suggest that students envision an elderly woman in a jumpsuit; a red umbrella; hot sun; two teenagers; a large dog.

Chapter 3   Your Autobiography

This chapter includes the following headings:
- What Is an Autobiography? (p. 39)
- Sample Autobiography: Helen Keller's *The Story of My Life* (p. 40)
- Researching Your Life Story (p. 42)
- Writing Your Life Story (p. 44)

In addition, 2 writing activities are included in this chapter.

THE AUTOBIOGRAPHY AND THE JOURNAL

An autobiography or an autobiographical sketch differs from a journal in several respects. These are some important differences:

1. An autobiography is a personal story about the past.
2. An autobiography addresses a large period of time—one's life to the time of writing.
3. An autobiography is written for others to read.
4. An autobiography has a narrative structure to the extent that a narrative is possible.
5. Autobiographies are carefully composed, revised, and corrected for other readers to enjoy.

THE AUTOBIOGRAPHICAL SKETCH

Since it would be impractical to ask students to write a complete autobiography for a classroom exercise, the focus of this unit is on the autobiographical sketch. In the text the student is offered a detailed strategy for gathering data about his or her life. The strategy covers the following:

1. Basic facts about your life
2. People
3. Places
4. Events

5. Things
6. Who I Am Today

Next, the student learns how to apply the 5Ws and H technique to organize important material for the autobiographical sketch.

Activities

1. The public library or your school library should have some excellent autobiographies to use with the class. Read excerpts from several of them to provide models for the students who will be writing an autobiographical sketch. When you do this, point out to students how each autobiographical writer has an individual writing voice.
2. If possible, show the short film *The Perfect Moment* (Pyramid Films, Santa Monica, California) to the class. In addition, or in lieu of showing the film, have students write a short autobiographical piece in which they recall "a perfect moment" from the past.
3. You may also wish to assign one or more of the following short autobiographical writing exercises:
   a. An Embarrassing Moment
   b. A Horrible Moment
   c. An Exciting Moment
   d. A Humorous Moment

   If you prefer to assign a more extensive project, have students compose a "Moments" anthology.
4. Invite a senior citizen to speak to your class. Ask the speaker to describe how school functioned when he or she was a student. Ask your guest to describe a memorable school experience. You may also wish to ask the speaker to sum up his or her life for the class. This oral type of autobiography can be very useful for stimulating interest in the whole process of autobiographical writing.

Chapter 4   The Personal Letter

This chapter includes the following headings:
- The Advantages of Personal Letters (p. 49)
- Planning a Personal Letter (p. 50)
- Personal Letter Formats (p. 53)
- Types of Personal Letters (p. 55)

In addition, 6 writing activities are placed throughout this chapter.

PERSONAL LETTERS

The personal letter requires effort to write. It is much easier to pick up a telephone and talk to a friend. Yet the effort and the expression that one puts into writing a personal letter make it an important means to enhance a relationship with another person.

The art of personal letter writing may well be disappearing in this society. Letters cost much more to mail than they did twenty years ago. Telephone rates, especially at discount times, are more reasonable than they were twenty years ago. Taking the time to write a letter seems to be more trouble than it was twenty years ago.

Indeed, writing a personal letter is like sending someone a gift of yourself. The thought and the time that it takes to write a personal letter are evidence that you care about the person to whom you are writing.

The text includes detailed instruction for planning a personal letter and for using the correct format for the letter. As with the journal and the autobiography, the 5Ws and H technique is used to stimulate thoughts to include in the letter. Students will find that writing personal letters provides good practice for developing a natural "writing voice." Also, there will be a built-in motivation when they are writing to people who will read and react to their letters.

Activities

1. Ask students to write a letter to someone who has made a difference in their lives—perhaps a parent, a grandparent, or another relative. It may be a friend. It may be someone who does not suspect that he or she has helped the student significantly. If the students wish to share these letters with the class, allow them to do so.

2. Initiate a pen pal club. The club may be on that corresponds with students from foreign countries. Or, you may choose to contact a school in another state and

ask for a list of students willing to correspond with your class members. This activity provides an interesting way to practice personal letter writing.

3. Ask students to write personal letters to authors whose books they have enjoyed. A student may choose to write to an author who is no longer living; however, if the author is living and the student can obtain his or her address from *Who's Who in America* or *Contemporary Authors*, the student should mail the letter. Often, an author can also be contacted through the publisher of his or her book.

Part 2   Paragraph Power: Developing Your Ideas Step by Step

GOALS

In Part 2, students will learn how to:
- select an effective topic for a paragraph.
- write effective topic sentences.
- use appropriate tone and unity in paragraphs.
- write effective titles for a group of paragraphs.
- write descriptive paragraphs.
- write narrative paragraphs.
- write expository paragraphs.
- write persuasive paragraphs.

Chapter 5 Writing Effective Paragraphs

This chapter includes the following headings:
- Selecting a Topic (p. 61)
- Topic Sentences (p. 62)
- Audience and Tone (p. 63)
- Unity in Paragraphs (p. 65)
- Effective Titles (p. 67)

In addition, 6 writing activities are placed throughout the chapter.

ELEMENTS OF EFFECTIVE PARAGRAPHS

In the text, the paragraph is defined as "a group of words that develop or explain a single idea." The paragraph is often a miniature model for more elaborate compositions. Without knowing how to develop appropriate, connected paragraphs, a student cannot write an effective composition.

This chapter covers the fundamentals for developing good paragraphs. Students begin by learning the function of the topic sentence. The topic sentence states a central idea that the other sentences develop or explain. This concept is one that must be clearly understood before paragraph writing can progress.

The other important elements of unity, audience, tone, and title are illustrated and developed in this chapter. Be certain that students clearly understand each of these concepts before proceeding. A careful beginning will smooth the road for swifter progress in effective paragraph writing.

Activities

1. Read model paragraphs to the class, but omit the topic sentence. Ask students to state the central idea of the paragraph.
2. Read excellent model paragraphs to students and point out why the topic sentence is effective.
3. Include an irrelevant sentence in a model paragraph that you read aloud to the class. Encourage students to discover how the irrelevant sentence destroys the unity of the paragraph.
4. Assemble a group of paragraphs that have been written for a variety of audiences (a formal paragraph, a political paragraph from a speech, a humorous paragraph, a paragraph from a friendly letter, a eulogy, an advertisement, etc.).

Discuss with students how the tones of the paragraphs differ from one another. This concept is very important, mainly because the audience for most student writing is the teacher. Students need to learn to write for a variety of audiences.
5. Read some model paragraphs from nonfiction and fiction. Ask students to give each paragraph a good title.

Chapter 6 Descriptive Paragraphs

This chapter includes the following headings:

- Descriptive Details (p. 69)
- Creating a Mood (p. 71)
- Sentence Order (p. 73)

In addition, 9 writing activities are placed throughout the chapter.

WRITING GOOD DESCRIPTIVE PARAGRAPHS

Learning to write descriptive paragraphs effectively is important for the beginning writer. The skill emphasizes specific writing that incorporates sense words such as those studied previously. You may wish to review the sense word lists in Chapter 2 (pp. 23–29).

This chapter uses exercises and activities, including Observation Notebook work, to show students how to develop an effective descriptive paragraph. The important concept to emphasize is that a descriptive paragraph paints a picture for the reader through verbal images. Learning how to use spatial order and to convey mood through details also are important skills.

Activities

1. Read examples of excellent descriptive writing. Ask students to note how the author uses vivid images and details to create a picture and a mood.
2. Ask the students to bring in examples of good descriptive writing from newspapers, magazines, and books. Share them with the class. Discuss why the writing is or is not effective.
3. Show the class slides or paintings that lend themselves to description. Ask students to list descriptive details about the visuals.

Chapter 7   Narrative Paragraphs

This chapter includes the following headings:
- Telling a Story (p. 79)
- Using Transitions (p. 83)

In addition, 6 writing activities are placed throughout the chapter.

WRITING GOOD NARRATIVE PARAGRAPHS

As discussed in the previous chapter, a descriptive paragraph paints a picture for the reader. A narrative paragraph, in contrast, tells a story. Students must learn the concept of *time* order to write an effective narrative paragraph. They must also learn to use transitions effectively. Although description can and should be used within a narrative paragraph when it is appropriate, the primary purpose of a narrative paragraph is to tell a story.

Narratives usually involve one or more main characters who face some sort of problem that needs to be solved. The problem is recognized and may or may not be solved. In "To Build a Fire," the problem is not solved, but the story is engrossing, nevertheless.

The narrative also begins at one place and ends in another, in order of time. The character or characters change somewhat during the narrative. Narrative writing can be as brief and unexciting as the nursery rhyme "Little Jack Horner" or as complex and lengthy as the novel *War and Peace*.

Activities

1. Ask students to bring in stories from a newspaper. Read the first one or two paragraphs of each. Discuss how the narrative elements emerge from these stories.
2. Read students one or two excellent short stories. Discuss how the narrative elements make the story effective. Emphasize how the author has used time order and description to make the story intriguing.
3. If possible, show students a short story that has been filmed. Discuss how the narrative elements emerge in the film. It would be a good exercise to have students read the actual short story to compare the two media.
4. Ask students to watch a television show and write the story in narrative form.
5. Ask students to bring in a photograph that depicts a character or characters about whom they can write a narrative paragraph.

Chapter 8   Expository Paragraphs

This chapter includes the following headings:
- Informing and Explaining (p. 87)
- Information in Order (p. 89)
- Explaining a Process (p. 92)
- Order of Importance (p. 96)

In addition, 8 writing activities are placed throughout the chapter.

WRITING GOOD EXPOSITORY PARAGRAPHS

Expository paragraphs inform or explain. Expository writing is the type of writing that students are required to do most often in classes in secondary school and college. For this reason, particular emphasis should be placed on understanding clearly how to develop expository paragraphs that reflect clear organization and careful thought.

In order to write exposition effectively, a student must learn to use transitions, to arrange information in order of time, to explain a process in clear steps, and to provide information in order of importance. All of these skills are introduced and reinforced in this chapter through writing activities. Additional activities such as those described below will serve to emphasize the concepts.

Activities

1. Ask students to explain a process. Some possibilities are these:
   a. How to change a tire
   b. How to mow a lawn
   c. How to wash dishes
   d. How to fry a hamburger
   e. How to tie a shoelace
2. Have students select five transitions and put them in time order. Then ask them to write an expository paragraph in which they use these transitions.
3. Read aloud examples of excellent expository paragraphs to the students. Discuss why the writing is effective and emphasize how the author achieved clarity in the presentation.

4. Show a process film. Most schools and public libraries have films on how to do something. Ask students to compose an expository piece of writing that conveys what the film presents.

Chapter 9   Persuasive Paragraphs

This chapter includes the following heading:

- Persuasion (p. 101)

In addition, 7 writing activities are placed throughout the chapter.

WRITING GOOD PERSUASIVE PARAGRAPHS

The purpose of a persuasive paragraph is to persuade the reader to accept the point of view of the writer. Being able to write persuasive paragraphs that support an opinion without injecting emotional fallacies and loaded rhetoric is a skill all students need to learn. This chapter trains students to plan a persuasive paragraph, organize it, and develop it competently. Students must learn to use transitions effectively within their paragraphs if their arguments are to be accepted.

Activities

1. Ask students to bring in editorials from newspapers or magazines. Read them aloud. Discuss how effective the editorials are and what makes them convincing or weak.
2. Ask students to select a controversial issue that is in the news. Have them write a persuasive paragraph that supports or attacks that issue.
3. Read aloud to the students some examples of excellent persuasive writing. Discuss how the author was able to convince the reader to support the opinion presented or how the author failed to do so.
4. Ask students to write a convincing advertisement for a mythical product.

Part 3   Longer Compositions: Writing for Others

GOALS

In Part 3, students will learn how to:

- select and narrow a subject for an essay.
- write a thesis statement and construct an outline for an essay.
- write several drafts and then a finished essay.
- write factual reports.
- incorporate research into a factual report.
- write a variety of reviews.
- write several kinds of business letters.
- construct a résumé.

Chapter 10 Writing an Essay

This chapter includes the following headings:
- Prewriting (p. 113)
- Prewriting and Research (p. 114)
- Thesis Statements (p. 115)
- The Outline (p. 115)
- The First Draft (p. 117)
- Selecting a Title (p. 123)
- Revising Your Rough Draft (p. 123)
- Writing and Proofreading Your Final Draft (p. 124)

In addition, 8 writing activities are placed throughout the chapter.

WRITING ESSAYS

This chapter is, in a sense, a tying together of what students have studied previously. Here, students will have an opportunity to apply their knowledge and demonstrate their understanding of the concepts presented thus far in the text.

This chapter develops instruction in the multiparagraph composition by illustrating the steps in writing an expository essay. The subject is first aid. First, prewriting is used to help the student discover how much he or she knows about the topic. Approaches to narrowing the subject and deciding upon a limited topic also are discussed.

When the student decides to write about the Heimlich maneuver, the text suggests resources for learning about the topic. The student then creates a thesis statement and constructs an outline from the prewriting activity, the research, and all the other pertinent knowledge he or she has accumulated.

After the outline is constructed, the student decides upon a five-paragraph organization for the composition. Next, he or she considers alternative introductions and reviews the use of transitions in the essay. The result is a first draft that comprises at least five paragraphs. The student then selects a title for the essay.

At this point, the student revises the rough draft, using the revision checklist provided (p. 124) as guidance. Finally, the final draft can be written and proofread.

This extended activity leads students through the steps involved in writing an expository composition. Remind students that the same process can be used for writing a descriptive composition, a narrative composition, or a persuasive composition. In addition, emphasize the importance of closely following the instructions for manuscript preparation and final proofreading.

Activities

1. Present a list of broad topics and ask each student to choose one as the topic for his or her five-paragraph essay. Remind the class to follow the steps that the students followed in writing the composition on the Heimlich maneuver.
2. Read excellent examples of various types of essays. Discuss the effectiveness of each of the examples.

Chapter 11 The Factual Report

This chapter includes the following headings:
- Planning a Factual Report (p. 127)
- Incorporating Research into a Factual Report (p. 132)

In addition, 8 writing activities are placed throughout the chapter.

REPORTS

This chapter presents a strategy for writing a factual report, provides short models of such reports, and includes activities that lead students through the writing of two reports. In doing so, this chapter reinforces many of the concepts taught in Chapter 10.

INCORPORATING RESEARCH

The second half of this chapter provides information and discusses procedures concerning the incorporation of research into a factual report. Students are instructed in how to conduct and organize research, how to take notes, and how to avoid plagiarism. Next, the focus moves to documenting a report, addressing the elements and placement of citations. Finally, a student learns how to compile a Works Cited page.

Activities

1. Ask class members to write a report about a topic currently in the news. Require that students use at least three different sources for information about their topic from the following group: newspapers, news magazines, television reports, radio reports.
2. Ask students to write a report about an event or issue at their school. Remind them to make special efforts to get facts and to document their sources.

Chapter 12　The Review

This chapter includes the following heading:

- Writing Reviews (p. 139)

In addition, 5 writing activities are placed throughout the chapter.

REVIEWS

Students frequently are required to write book reports and reviews. This chapter outlines techniques for reviewing a book, a movie, or a play. Again, the 5Ws and H technique is used to focus upon the important elements of the work. Two fables are used to illustrate the technique: "The Turtle and the Rabbit" and "The Sun and the Wind."

These illustrations lead to an extensive analysis of a review of "The Tell-Tale Heart" by Edgar Allan Poe. Students are asked questions about the story before they read it. These questions concern the title, the setting, characters, plot, style, theme, and impact.

Students are then asked to read Poe's popular story. Answers to the previously asked questions are provided. A model review of the story illustrates how a student might use the information given in responses to these questions to write the composition. Finally, to reinforce their understanding, students are asked to select a short story and to write a review of it, according to the guidelines given in the chapter.

The final instruction in the chapter shows how students can apply many of the same techniques in writing a book report, a movie review, or a play review. In fact, the use of the short story as a basis for teaching students how to review a book was a practical choice. The short story contains the necessary elements for reviewing, but in a compressed form.

Activities

1. Students should read the book reviews in the Sunday newspaper or a weekly magazine and select one example of a well-written review to share with the class. How does the review encourage the reader to read the book?
2. Assign a movie for review. The students may watch it either on television or in a theater.
3. Share good examples of movie reviews with the class. Discuss the qualities that make the reviews effective.

Chapter 13   Business Communications

This chapter includes the following headings:
- The Importance of Business Communication (p. 154)
- The Business Letter (p. 154)
- Addressing Mail (p. 157)
- Letters of Inquiry (p. 159)
- Letters to Colleges (p. 160)
- Letters of Complaint (p. 162)
- Letters of Application (p. 163)
- Writing a Résumé (p. 165)
- Application Forms (p. 166)

In addition, 9 writing activities are placed throughout the chapter.

BUSINESS LETTERS

Students sometimes do not appreciate the importance of using acceptable form and style for business letters. This chapter provides examples of proper formats for business letters. Students also are instructed in writing clearly and directly and with a polite tone.

Activities

1. Contact some businesses in your community to ask for samples of correspondence to show students. To make the activity even more productive, try to identify weaknesses as well as strengths in the sample letters.
2. Ask students to bring in letters to the editor from magazines and newspapers so that the class may critique them.

APPLICATIONS AND RÉSUMÉS

The ability to fill out an application form correctly and neatly and to construct a complete, concise résumé are skills many students assume they naturally possess. When faced with doing so, however, many students discover their need for additional instruction.

Activities

1. Contact some businesses in your community and ask them to provide you with application forms. Use these to help students practice appropriate responses to a variety of questions.

2. Ask students to interview a businessperson about how he or she goes about interviewing and hiring a job candidate. In particular, students should ask questions about letters of application, résumés, and application forms. To conclude, require students to write a report on the interview to share with the class.

3. Invite some business executives to visit your class and talk to students about how their businesses operate and what they are looking for when they hire employees. You may be surprised at the willingness of many executives to share their experience. Community organizations such as the Rotary, the Lions, and the Exchange can help you find resource people. In addition, the Chamber of Commerce may also offer information.

Part 4 Language Skills Review: A Quick Reference for Correct Usage Answer Key

Chapter 14 Sentence Sense

SKILLS ACTIVITY 1: ARRANGING WORDS FOR SENTENCE SENSE, p. 173

1. <u>Ramona</u> <u>took</u> Juan to the movies last night.
2. The <u>cat</u> <u>meowed</u> because it was hungry.
3. The <u>dog</u> <u>barked</u> at the stranger on the street.
4. <u>George</u> <u>enjoyed</u> eating the ice cream cone.
5. <u>Sally</u> <u>played</u> tennis with her friend.

SKILLS ACTIVITY 2: FINDING SUBJECTS AND PREDICATES, p. 174

1. <u>"Garfield"</u> has remained a favorite for many years.
2. <u>Another popular comic</u> is "Peanuts."
3. <u>"Cathy"</u> has stayed in top place, too.
4. <u>Children</u> have been comic fans since the beginning.
5. <u>Many adults</u> read one or more comics daily.
6. <u>Daily readers</u> include about forty percent adults.
7. <u>Story-telling comic strips</u> seem on the way out.
8. <u>Humorous comics</u> have become more and more popular.
9. <u>The popular strips</u> are becoming funnier each year.
10. <u>Many people</u> buy newspapers because of their comics.

SKILLS ACTIVITY 3: REPLACING SUBJECTS, p. 175

Answers will vary. The first sentence might be written in a variety of ways, for example:

<u>All the television stations</u> carried the election returns.
Only <u>*The Morning Herald*</u> carried the election returns.

40 Writing by Doing

SKILLS ACTIVITY 4: REPLACING PREDICATES, p. 175

Answers will vary. The first sentence might be written in a variety of ways, for example:

A sudden freeze <u>can cause pipes to crack.</u>
A sudden freeze <u>can make driving hazardous.</u>

SKILLS ACTIVITY 5: WRITING SENTENCES WITH COMPOUND SUBJECTS AND VERBS, p. 176

Answers will vary. For example, the first sentence can be expanded into a compound subject in numerous ways:

<u>She and her dog</u> fell knee-deep into the mud.
<u>She and all the groceries</u> fell knee-deep into the mud.

The sixth sentence can be given the following compound verbs, for example:

Her escort <u>lost the tickets for the show and dripped gravy on his tie.</u>
My mother <u>lost the tickets for the show and forgot her house key.</u>

SKILLS ACTIVITY 6: WRITING COMPOUND SENTENCES, p. 177

Answers will vary. The first sentence could be written as follows:

A tiny calculator does problems instantly and it's easy to carry around.
A tiny calculator does problems but sometimes the small keys make it difficult to use efficiently.

SKILLS ACTIVITIES 7–19: SENTENCE PATTERNS, pp. 179–185

This section deals with the four most commonly used sentence patterns. Of the four, the noun-verb pattern is the basic pattern for the majority of all written sentences. The effective writer, however, will vary his or her sentence structure to maintain the reader's interest and to create an interesting rhythm.

An important point for students to understand is that the basic patterns are just that—basic. Each pattern can be expanded with subordinate clauses, with the connection of two main clauses by a conjunction, and through a variety of other insertions, additions, and amplifications.

Example: Bill, the captain of the football team, enjoyed pizza more than any other food in the world, but when he was a child, his mother would not allow him to eat cheese, so he went absolutely wild when he visited the pizza parlor and gorged himself on delicious tomato and cheese pies, much to the distress of his coach, who sat unobserved in the corner, sipping a diet cola and wondering about the biggest game of the year that was looming in his mind and was crucial to the team's playoff chances.

This sentence, of course, is much too long. The writing would be more effective if it were broken up into several shorter sentences.

Example: Bill, the captain of the football team, enjoyed pizza more than any other food in the world. When he was a child, his mother would not allow him to eat cheese. He went absolutely wild when he visited the pizza parlor. He gorged himself on delicious tomato and cheese pies. This distressed his coach, who sat unobserved in the corner. The coach sipped a diet cola. He wondered about the biggest game of the year. It loomed in his mind because the game was crucial to the team's playoff chances.

Five of the eight sentences in this paragraph are the basic noun-verb pattern that includes expansions and modifiers. Breaking up the original paragraph into shorter sentences makes the paragraph more readable.

Be careful, however, to emphasize to students that these patterns are not the only ways sentences can be written. Each pattern can be expanded with modifiers. Nonetheless, these basic patterns will show the fundamental structures for most sentences.

Activities

1. Ask each student to clip a story from a newspaper or a magazine. Collect the stories and read examples of the noun-verb pattern. You might also wish to show how the noun-verb pattern is the basis for the sentence, but that frequently it is expanded through modification and connection. Save the stories in order to do this with the other patterns in this section as well.
2. Ask students to write a paragraph of at least seven sentences with only a noun and a verb for each sentence. Allow them to use *the*, *a*, and *an*. This exercise illustrates how basic the noun-verb pattern is for communication and also how

lean and repetitive the noun-verb pattern is when it is not modified and expanded.
3. Ask students to write five sentences that are basic noun-verb patterns, noun-verb-noun patterns, or noun-verb-noun-noun patterns. Have them scramble the sentences. Next, organize the students into pairs. Partners should then exchange the scrambled sentences and reorganize them into proper sentences.

NOUN–LINKING VERB–NOUN PATTERN AND THE NOUN–LINKING VERB–ADJECTIVE PATTERN

It is important to learn the linking verbs. Students should memorize them. Knowing the linking verbs helps immensely when grammar is discussed and when writing is analyzed. One test of the noun-linking verb-noun pattern is that the subject is the same as the complement.

Examples: The bird is a duck. (*Bird* and *duck* are the same.)
    Paul became a priest. (*Paul* and *priest* are the same.)

In a noun-linking verb-adjective pattern, the adjective at the end modifies the subject.

Examples: Alice appeared happy. (happy Alice)
    Milton became blind. (blind Milton)

Activities

1. Ask students to write a paragraph of seven sentences using only noun-linking verb-noun patterns and noun-linking verb-adjective patterns. This will be a challenge, but it can be done.
2. Ask students to write three sentences in the noun-linking verb-noun pattern and three sentences in the noun-linking verb-adjective pattern. Then ask them to scramble the sentences. Organize the students into pairs and have them exchange their written sentences. Each student should reorganize the scrambled sentences into proper sentences.
3. Using stories from newspapers or magazines, give the students illustrations of the above patterns.

SKILLS ACTIVITIES 20–21: RUN-ON SENTENCES AND SENTENCE FRAGMENTS, pp. 187–189

These two errors are the most common errors in student writing (with the exception of misspelled words). To correct run-on sentences, students must understand that a comma is not a connector for two sentences. They must recognize conjunctions and their functions. To correct sentence fragments, students must understand that a subject must have a verb to complete a sentence, or a verb or verb form must have a subject if it is to be a sentence.

A good way to begin the study of the run-on sentence is to study conjunctions. Give students many examples of coordinating conjunctions connecting two sentences.

Activities

1. Ask students to write five sentences that use the conjunction *and* to connect them. Then, ask them to write five sentences that use the following conjunctions: *or*, *but*, *nor*, *for*, and *yet*. After they have written these, show what happens when you take out the conjunction and insert a comma.

   Example: I enjoy chili, but I like vegetable soup better.
   I enjoy chili, I like vegetable soup better. (run-on)

2. Ask students to memorize the conjunctive adverbs. Ask them to write sentences that use each conjunctive adverb. Demonstrate how the semicolon functions as a connector with the conjunctive adverb.

   Examples: I enjoy chili; also, I like vegetable soup.
   I am very poor at sports; consequently, I do not play football.

   Commonly used conjunctive adverbs are *accordingly, also, besides, consequently, furthermore, hence, however, moreover, nevertheless, therefore, thus,* and *still*.

   To connect the sentence fragment, teach students to ask two important questions as a test of a complete sentence:

   - Who or what is doing something?
   - What is the actor doing?

   Example: A beautiful day in the country. (fragment)
   George enjoyed a beautiful day in the country. (Who? George. What? George enjoyed.)

3. Ask students to write down five subjects—people or things. Ask them to explain why these are not sentences. Ask them to make them into sentences.

4. Ask students to write down five verbs or verb phrases. As a class, discuss why these are not sentences. Ask them to make them into sentences.

SKILL TEST 1: FINDING SUBJECTS AND VERBS, p. 189

Copy each sentence below and underline the subject or subjects once and the verb or verbs twice. Watch for compound sentences.

1. <u>Daylight Savings Time</u> <u>continues</u> for more than half the year.
2. High-speed <u>railroads</u> <u>connect</u> major cities in Europe and <u>make</u> traveling to different countries very easy.
3. Car <u>accidents</u> and automobile <u>deaths</u> <u>decrease</u> with lower speed limits.
4. <u>Charles Lindbergh</u> <u>flew</u> across the Atlantic alone and <u>he</u> later <u>wrote</u> several books about his experience.
5. Many <u>people</u> <u>have been eating</u> and <u>cooking</u> Chinese foods lately.
6. <u>Mexico City</u> <u>has</u> a lot to offer tourists but <u>it</u> <u>is</u> also very polluted.
7. <u>Rain</u> <u>can</u> both <u>nurture</u> and <u>destroy</u> crops.
8. The <u>number</u> of smokers and drinkers <u>has been decreasing</u>.
9. <u>Traffic</u> <u>has become</u> lighter with higher fuel costs.
10. <u>Matilda</u> <u>doesn't want</u> to go with us nor <u>does</u> <u>she</u> <u>want</u> us to call.

SKILL TEST 2: IDENTIFYING SENTENCE PATTERNS, pp. 189–190

1. Noun-verb-adverb
2. Noun-verb-noun-completer
3. Noun-linking verb-adjective
4. Noun-verb-noun-completer
5. Noun-verb-adverb
6. Noun-verb-adverb
7. Noun-linking verb-noun
8. Noun-linking verb-adjective
9. Noun-verb-noun
10. Noun-linking verb-adjective

SKILL TEST 3: IDENTIFYING AND CORRECTING RUN-ONS AND FRAGMENTS, p. 190

1. run on
2. fragment
3. run on
4. run on
5. fragment
6. fragment
7. run on
8. run on
9. fragment
10. fragment

Chapter 15 Building Sentences with Phrases and Clauses

SKILLS ACTIVITY 1: ADDING PREPOSITIONAL PHRASES TO THE SUBJECT, p. 193

1. Nearly everyone in the U.S. watches the weather.
2. Some people with mathematical skills really understand computers.
3. Other people besides outdoor workers experience physical discomforts on the job.
4. Baseball or football fans are very interested during the season.
5. Most residents of northern areas watch the winter weather.
6. A heavy snow can happen very quickly during winter months.
7. A temperature variation of just one degree can mean the difference between rain and snow.
8. One degree on the Celsius scale makes an even greater difference.
9. The hurricane season is closely watched in summer and fall.
10. The weather bureau picnic on a rainy day is a classic joke.

SKILLS ACTIVITY 2: ADDING PREPOSITIONAL PHRASES TO THE PREDICATE, p. 194

1. A TV forecaster gives the statistics of temperature and precipitation.
2. The forecast includes data about approaching conditions.
3. The anchorperson usually makes an opening remark about yesterday's weather.
4. The forecaster begins the presentation with a satellite photo.
5. The photo shows weather systems in much of the nation.
6. Next he or she gives a forecast for the next 24 hours.
7. The segment ends with a prediction for the next five days.
8. No one can trust a forecast beyond one full day.
9. Some conditions can make a forecaster only a good guesser of any weather.
10. Rain or sleet or snow is often the prediction throughout the mid-Atlantic region.

SKILLS ACTIVITY 3: ADDING PREPOSITIONAL PHRASES TO SENTENCES, p. 194

Answers will vary. For example the first sentence could be rewritten as follows:

The National Weather Service provides basic data for use in predicting tornadoes.

SKILLS ACTIVITY 4: PLACING ADVERB PREPOSITIONAL PHRASES, p. 196

1. A robot is designed with flexible arms and hands.
2. Like a human hand, the mechanical hand can grasp with great precision.
3. Some 5000 robots already are working in factories.
4. A robot may pick up and insert parts into complex machinery.
5. Or, it can unload items from packing cases.
6. Some robots can actually see with TV camera "eyes."
7. A seeing robot matches images and objects with its eyes.
8. It then selects the objects from an assembly line without any mistakes.
9. Another robot can grind and polish surfaces with efficiency and care.
10. Specially designed robots can reach into difficult places.

SKILLS ACTIVITY 5: ADDING ADVERB PREPOSITIONAL PHRASES, p. 197

Answers will vary. For example, the first sentence could be rewritten as follows:

Another robot can weld and paint while the adhesive is drying.

SKILLS ACTIVITY 6: PLACING ADVERB INFINITIVE PHRASES, pp. 198–199

1. Months ahead of time a family began to plan their trip.
2. Their early start was needed to get a reservation.
3. The reservation was made to exchange houses.
4. Another family in Europe had also planned to do the same thing.

48 Writing by Doing

5. The two families wrote letters to arrange the exchange.
6. At vacation time the American family traveled to stay in the house in Europe.
7. The European family made the trip to use the house in the U.S.
8. Both families were ready to take good care of the houses.
9. In fact, they were eager to please one another.
10. Everyone was happy to save on hotel bills.

SKILLS ACTIVITY 7: ADDING ADVERB INFINITIVE PHRASES, p. 199

Answers will vary. For example, the first sentence could be rewritten as follows:

Each family started early to avoid being disappointed.

SKILLS ACTIVITY 8: PLACING ADJECTIVE INFINITIVE PHRASES, pp. 199–200

1. Bills to be spent stay in circulation until worn out.
2. Money to be deposited is brought into the banks.
3. However, the money to be saved is now in larger bills than one dollar.
4. The everyday money to be used as change is more and more in dollar bills than in coins.
5. Bills to be inspected are set aside in the bank.
6. Special new machines to inspect paper money are being used.
7. Worn-out bills to be destroyed are put into a shredding machine.
8. The better bills to be recirculated are paid out by the tellers.
9. The one-dollar coin to spend every day never caught on.
10. Perhaps the two-dollar bill to use for many purposes will grow more popular.

SKILLS ACTIVITY 9: ADDING ADJECTIVE INFINITIVE PHRASES, p. 200

1. Late in 1963 the president issued an order to make a new coin.
2. The Kennedy half-dollar became an instantly popular coin to collect.
3. Many people collected the 1964 all-silver coin to keep as a souvenir.
4. Other people collected these silver coins to melt down into metal.
5. Artisans used the handsome coins to be worn in jewelry.
6. A number of the coins were made into charms to be worn on bracelets.
7. Many of these half-dollars did not stay in circulation to be spent.
8. The latest issues of the coin contain no silver to be melted down.
9. These later coins have the same value to be used as money.
10. Yet they are still very handsome coins to keep and admire.

SKILLS ACTIVITY 10: ADDING PARTICIPIAL PHRASES TO THE SUBJECT, pp. 201–202

1. People lacking travel know-how can bring too many things.
2. Other travelers knowing of emergencies carry needed supplies.
3. Travelers visiting large cities do need detailed maps.
4. Some people accustomed to power blackouts carry extra candles.
5. One woman disliking stuffy rooms always brings air freshener.
6. A particular person avoiding fast-food places takes his own packaged foods.
7. Some people following strict diets must carry all their food supplies.
8. Pet owners attached to their animals may bring them along.
9. Special carriers designed for their safety are available for pets.
10. Many pets accustomed to their secure homes are poor travelers.

SKILLS ACTIVITY 11: ADDING PARTICIPIAL PHRASES TO THE PREDICATE, p. 202

1. Most people can pack extra coat hangers taking little space.
2. Frequent travelers carry schedule books giving flight information.

3. Smart travelers bring a first-aid kit filled with medical supplies.
4. Every traveler's friend is drip-dry clothing needing no ironing.
5. Instant coffee is handy for small hotels lacking room service.
6. Another handy item is an immersion heater providing hot water.
7. One gourmet always carries a picnic basket packed with favorite foods.
8. A helpful travel item is some spray cleaner designed for spot cleaning.
9. Early risers use a small alarm clock intended for travel.
10. Some even carry a sewing kit filled with pins and buttons.

SKILLS ACTIVITY 12: ADDING PARTICIPIAL PHRASES TO SENTENCES, pp. 202–203

Answers will vary. For example, the first sentence could be rewritten as follows:

New products to tempt young children always are available.

SKILLS ACTIVITY 13: ADDING ADJECTIVE CLAUSES TO THE SUBJECT, pp. 204–205

1. An ancient ledger that is 3000 years old is in fairly good shape.
2. The paper that is used in a book makes all the difference.
3. Modern paper that has lots of acid destroys itself over the years.
4. Most publications that were printed since 1850 cannot last very long.
5. Many items that were printed since 1900 have already disintegrated.
6. A book that is published today has a life expectancy of about 50 years.
7. People who care about books could do something about this.
8. Publishers who want to preserve their work could use nonacid paper.
9. Specialists who are experts could preserve valuable books on film.
10. The amount of money that would be needed is a problem.

SKILLS ACTIVITY 14: ADDING ADJECTIVE CLAUSES TO THE PREDICATE, p. 205

1. Fossils are the remains of animals and vegetables that have been preserved.
2. Over 100 years ago scientists began digging up fossils that are studied today.
3. Museums store these fossils, which are irreplaceable.
4. Museum storage vaults are watched over by scientists who classified the fossils.
5. These fossils have often been inaccessible even to students who would like to study them.
6. However, the fossils are available to something that cannot be locked out.
7. The fossils have gradually been eaten into by the air which is acid-filled.
8. The air destroys dinosaur bones that had been buried for 100 million years.
9. Yet, you cannot blame the museum people who are trying to preserve their treasures.
10. Throughout the land, more fossils are destroyed by bulldozers and plows that chew into the earth.

SKILLS ACTIVITY 15: ADDING ADJECTIVE CLAUSES TO SENTENCES, p. 206

Answers will vary. For example the first sentence could be rewritten as follows:

A new kind of shampoo is called Dandy Ruff, guaranteed to be tough on dandruff.

SKILLS ACTIVITY 16: ADDING ADVERB CLAUSES TO SENTENCES, p. 208

Answers will vary. For example, the first sentence could be rewritten as follows:

Littering is not the only problem after the outdoor rock concert.

SKILLS ACTIVITY 17: INSERTING ADVERB CLAUSES IN SENTENCES, pp. 208–209

Answers will vary. For example, the first sentence could be rewritten as follows:

Before fines are imposed, your area can clean up litter.

SKILLS ACTIVITY 18: COMBINING PHRASES AND CLAUSES TO EXPAND SENTENCES, p. 209

Answers will vary. For example, the first sentence could be written as follows:

People drive on the expressways.
People drive on the expressways at great speed.
People drive on the expressways at great speed as if they were crazy.

SKILL TEST 1: PHRASES, p. 210

1. A good pitcher may not be good (prepositional) <u>at hitting</u>.
2. The expressway has a special lane (prepositional) <u>for fast traffic</u>.
3. Everyone was too tired <u>to stay up</u> (infinitive) (prepositional) <u>for the late show</u>.
4. A course <u>teaching first aid</u> (participial) is a must <u>for campers</u> (prepositional).
5. The best shows <u>to watch</u> (infinitive) often are reruns <u>of old movies</u> (prepositional).
6. Many stores sell gourmet foods (participial) <u>displayed in a special department</u>.
7. A fresh coat of paint may be all (infinitive) that is needed <u>to make a table look like new</u>.
8. The exit ramp is the last one (prepositional) <u>before the tollgate</u>.
9. Energy-saving measures should be (prepositional) taken <u>in every household</u>.
10. Many people will shop for a long (prepositional) (infinitive) time <u>for a good bargain</u> <u>to take home</u>.

SKILL TEST 2: CLAUSES, p. 210

1. Your skin needs protection
   (adverb)
   while you are in the sun.
2. Before the speech ended, people began leaving.
3. Radio was once the major enter-
   (adjective)
   tainment medium that drew millions of listeners every day.
   (adverb)
4. Hang gliding is dangerous whenever wind conditions are uncertain.
   (adjective)
5. A men's jacket style that is always in fashion is called the blazer.
6. There are cosmetic products
   (adjective)
   that are made for teenage skin problems.
   (adjective)
7. The TV personalities who get high audience ratings stay on the air.
8. Plain old blue jeans were popular
   (adverb)
   before designer labels came in fashion.
9. You pay for "free" TV through
   (adjective)
   advertisements that persuade you to buy.
   (adverb)
10. When the political conventions end, the election campaign begins.

SKILL TEST 3: IDENTIFYING PHRASES AND CLAUSES, p. 211

1. Preventive maintenance means
   (adjective)
   solving repair problems (before
   (preposition)
   they become serious.)
   (preposition)
2. A banner headline (across the
   (adjective)
   front page) announced who had won the election.
   (adjective)
3. The American hotdog which is a favorite at ballgames was cre-
   (preposition)
   ated in Germany (before becoming a fast-food dish.)
4. Solar energy collectors work
   (adverb)
   only where there is plenty of
   (infinitive)
   sunshine (to activate them.)
   (adjective)
5. Jet planes, which can go faster than the speed of sound, have
   (adjective)
   changed the way we travel.
6. Chicago was the nation's rail
   (adverb)
   transportation center before truck and air freight were important.

7. Products <u>that were unknown ten years ago</u> (adjective) are now everyday items.
8. A weekend <u>when the weather's stormy</u> (adverb) is a great time <u>to catch up</u> (infinitive) (on reading.) (preposition)
9. Everyone was interested (in the championship game) (preposition) <u>seen on cable TV</u>. (adjective)
10. (During the winter months,) (preposition) (for Caribbean cruises) (preposition) attract the eye of travelers <u>who can afford to pay the airfare</u> (adjective) (for a week in the sun.) (preposition)

Chapter 16   Verb Power

SKILLS ACTIVITY 1: ACTIVE VERBS, p. 214

1. need
2. should save
3. risk
4. have improved
5. can show
6. attack
7. approved
8. have been learning
9. can harm
10. earned

SKILLS ACTIVITY 2: PASSIVE VERSUS ACTIVE VERBS, pp. 215–216

Active verbs:
1. met
2. included
3. began
4. would attend
5. slammed
6. walked
7. shaking

Passive verbs:
1. were given
2. was introduced
3. had not been told

SKILLS ACTIVITY 3: CHANGING PASSIVE VERBS TO ACTIVE, pp. 216–217

1. The cowhands stampeded the herd.
2. Abraham passed the test.
3. Nancy shoveled the snow.
4. I am winning the game.
5. The trick fooled you.
6. The flea bit the dog.
7. The host served dinner to the guests.
8. The campers lit the fire.
9. A tough cowhand road a fierce bull.
10. The surprise party delighted his aunt.

SKILLS ACTIVITY 4: FINDING LINKING VERBS, p. 219

1. are
2. appears
3. remains
4. look
5. became
6. remains
7. taste
8. feel
9. sound
10. became

SKILLS ACTIVITY 5: EXCHANGING ONE LINKING VERB FOR ANOTHER, pp. 219–220

1. Predicting weather is scientific.
2. Actually it seems more an art than a science.
3. Scientific information remains important to a weather forecaster.
4. Yet, exact weather information often becomes doubtful.
5. In many areas, rain, snow, and fog are impossible to predict.
6. Sometimes the atmosphere almost becomes snowy.
7. Also, the sky appears a certain way during tornado conditions.
8. Some storms actually feel musty.
9. Before a snow, the air feels deadened.
10. Weather prediction often remains good guesswork.

SKILLS ACTIVITY 6: FINDING COMPLETE VERBS, p. 222

Placement may vary.

1. World-famous people were definitely making the voyage.
2. People had never questioned the safety of the ship.
3. The vessel had been faultlessly designed as "unsinkable."
4. The ship was actually traveling through iceberg-filled waters.
5. A huge iceberg scraped beside the ship.
6. The iceberg was cutting lengthwise into the ship like a can opener.
7. Desperately, passengers ran for the lifeboats.
8. Many of the boats unfortunately had become stuck.
9. The situation steadily worsened for the next two hours.
10. Then the unsinkable *Titanic* quickly did sink.

SKILLS ACTIVITY 7: ADDING ADVERBS TO COMPLETE VERBS, pp. 222–223

Some possible responses:

1. The early trans-Atlantic travelers drifted slowly.
2. The trip could frequently take several weeks.
3. Later the steamship gradually took passengers to Europe.
4. The steamship trip would eventually take several days.
5. Steamships could certainly be elegant and luxurious.
6. Some of them actually seemed more like floating palaces.
7. However, they also had become expensive.
8. Today only a few of them ever cross the sea.
9. A regular jet actually makes the crossing in seven hours.
10. A supersonic jet can make the trip sometimes in three hours.

SKILL TEST 1: DISTINGUISHING BETWEEN THE FOUR VERB TYPES, p. 223

1. Usually <u>governments</u> <u>add</u> sales taxes onto goods. (active)
2. <u>Fog</u> <u>can move</u> quickly across the water. (complete)
3. Properly frozen <u>meats</u> and <u>vegetables</u> <u>taste</u> perfectly fresh. (linking)
4. Each year the <u>sky</u> <u>becomes</u> more crowded with aircraft. (linking)
5. <u>Lady Ashton</u> <u>was given</u> a yacht for her birthday. (passive)
6. Sometimes <u>they</u> <u>don't show</u> up for appointments. (complete)
7. At that exact moment, the <u>photographer</u> <u>snapped</u> a picture of the eclipse. (active)
8. Thin, melting <u>ice</u> on a lake <u>appears</u> discolored. (linking)
9. The <u>price</u> of coffee <u>has risen</u> dramatically during the winter. (complete)
10. The <u>television set</u> <u>was stolen</u> right under our noses by a masked thief. (passive)

SKILL TEST 2: CONVERTING PASSIVE VERBS INTO ACTIVE, p. 223

1. The company normally ships the goods every Monday morning.
2. Our friends treated us to a steak.
3. The green and white team has won the game.
4. Most of the people considered the leader outstanding.
5. Attentive and competent waiters always serve superb food in a five-star restaurant.
6. Did a falling tree injure Phillip?
7. Stefanie hasn't sent me a letter in over a month.
8. Your admirers obviously supported you strongly.
9. The newspaper accidentally revealed the name of the winner.
10. You must give your bid before the end of the day.

Chapter 17   Troublesome Verbs

SKILLS ACTIVITY 1: GROUP A:
begin, blow, bring, burst, buy, p. 227

1. began
2. blown
3. brought
4. burst
5. bought
6. begun
7. blown
8. brought
9. burst
10. buys

SKILLS ACTIVITY 2: GROUP B:
catch, choose, come, cost, do, drink, p. 228

1. caught
2. chosen
3. come
4. cost
5. done
6. drank
7. caught
8. chose
9. come
10. done

SKILLS ACTIVITY 3: GROUP C:
drive, eat, fall, feel, fly, p. 229

1. drove
2. eaten
3. fallen
4. felt
5. flown
6. driven
7. ate
8. fallen
9. felt
10. flown

SKILLS ACTIVITY 4: GROUP D:
freeze, give, go, grow, know, pp. 230–231

1. frozen
2. given
3. gone
4. grew
5. known
6. froze
7. gave
8. gone
9. grown
10. knew

SKILLS ACTIVITY 5: GROUP E:
lead, lend, lie, lose, make, put, p. 232

1. led
2. lent
3. lies
4. lost
5. made
6. put
7. leading
8. lent
9. lain
10. made

SKILLS ACTIVITY 6: GROUP F:
ride, ring, rise, run, say, p. 233

1. ridden
2. rung
3. risen
4. run
5. said
6. rode
7. rung
8. rose
9. run
10. say

SKILLS ACTIVITY 7: GROUP G:
see, set, shrink, sing, sit, p. 234

1. saw
2. set
3. shrunk
4. sang
5. set
6. seen
7. shrank
8. sung
9. sat
10. sat

SKILLS ACTIVITY 8: GROUP H:
speak, steal, swim, take, teach, p. 236

1. spoken
2. stolen
3. swam
4. taken
5. taught
6. spoke
7. stole
8. swum
9. took
10. taught

SKILLS ACTIVITY 9: GROUP I:
tear, think, throw, wear, write, p. 237

1. torn
2. thought
3. thrown
4. worn
5. written
6. tore
7. thought
8. thrown
9. worn
10. writing

SKILLS ACTIVITY 10: *may/can*, p. 238

1. can
2. may
3. may
4. might
5. could
6. May
7. may
8. might, might
9. could
10. can, Can

SKILLS ACTIVITY 11: *let/leave*, p. 239

1. let
2. let
3. left
4. let
5. Leave

SKILLS ACTIVITY 12: *lie/lay*, p. 240

1. Lie
2. Lay
3. lay
4. lain
5. laid
6. lay
7. laid
8. lie
9. lying
10. laying

SKILLS ACTIVITY 13: *rise/raise*, p. 241

1. raised
2. rose
3. rose
4. raise
5. risen
6. raised
7. rise
8. raise
9. risen
10. rising

SKILLS ACTIVITY 14: *set/sit*, p. 242

1. sit
2. set
3. sit
4. set
5. sat
6. sat
7. set
8. sitting
9. set
10. sat

SKILLS ACTIVITY 15: *teach/learn*, p. 243

1. teach
2. learn
3. learned
4. learned
5. learned
6. learn
7. teach
8. learn
9. Learning
10. learned

SKILLS ACTIVITY 16: FORMS OF *be*, p. 245

1. Are
2. was
3. are
4. Were
5. are
6. will be
7. shall be
8. Were
9. were
10. were

SKILL TEST 1: IRREGULAR VERBS, pp. 246–247

1. bring
2. burst
3. caught
4. came
5. done
6. drunk
7. drove
8. eaten
9. feels
10. given
11. gone
12. grew
13. froze
14. lost
15. put
16. made
17. bought
18. chose
19. led
20. lain
21. ridden
22. rung
23. rise
24. run
25. say
26. set
27. shrank
28. sang
29. sitting
30. spoke
31. stole
32. swum
33. took
34. taught
35. torn
36. thought
37. threw
38. worn
39. written
40. saw

SKILL TEST 2: CONFUSING VERBS, p. 247

1. May
2. can
3. let
4. leave
5. lie
6. lay
7. raised
8. rose
9. sit

10. set
11. teach
12. taught
13. is
14. Are
15. were
16. were
17. will be
18. was
19. were
20. Were

Chapter 18   Using Correct Pronouns

SKILLS ACTIVITY 1: USING CORRECT PRONOUNS, pp. 250–251

1. it
2. Charlie and I
3. We
4. She
5. Benita and she
6. him
7. Between you and me
8. them
9. They
10. it

SKILLS ACTIVITY 2: USING POSSESSIVE PRONOUNS, pp. 251–252

1. its
2. her
3. our
4. mine
5. my
6. yours
7. their
8. his
9. hers
10. ours

SKILLS ACTIVITY 3: USING INDEFINITE PRONOUNS, p. 253

1. he or she
2. its
3. their
4. his or her
5. its
6. their
7. their
8. his
9. its
10. his or her
11. its
12. his or her
13. his or her
14. his or her
15. their
16. their
17. their
18. its
19. his or her
20. his or her

SKILLS ACTIVITY 4: USING REFLEXIVE PRONOUNS, p. 254

1. myself
2. yourself
3. himself
4. herself
5. itself
6. yourselves
7. ourselves
8. themselves
9. yourself
10. itself

SKILLS ACTIVITY 5: USING INTERROGATIVE PRONOUNS, p. 255

1. Who
2. Whom
3. Which
4. Whose
5. What

SKILLS ACTIVITY 6: CHOOSING *who* OR *whom*, p. 255

1. Who
2. Who
3. Who
4. whom
5. Who

SKILLS ACTIVITY 7: USING DEMONSTRATIVE PRONOUNS, p. 256

1. This
2. These
3. Those
4. That
5. These

SKILLS ACTIVITY 8: USING RELATIVE PRONOUNS, pp. 256–257

1. that
2. who
3. whom
4. whose
5. that
6. which
7. who
8. whose
9. that
10. that

SKILL TEST: USING CORRECT PRONOUNS, p. 257

1. his
2. She and I
3. himself
4. his or her
5. who
6. her
7. me
8. He and I
9. that
10. his or her
11. Who
12. These
13. we
14. their
15. whom
16. I
17. his
18. I
19. who

Chapter 19   Subject-Verb Agreement

SKILLS ACTIVITY 1: SIMPLE SUBJECT AND VERBS, p. 259

1. works
2. finishes
3. is
4. wants
5. break
6. plays
7. puzzles
8. need
9. bark
10. loves

SKILLS ACTIVITY 2: SUBJECTS WITH PREDICATE NOMINATIVES, p. 260

1. was
2. are
3. seem
4. are
5. were
6. was
7. was
8. were
9. are
10. seem

SKILLS ACTIVITY 3: SUBJECTS WITH PREPOSITIONAL PHRASES, p. 261

1. knows
2. is
3. make
4. know
5. is
6. learn
7. knows
8. like
9. has
10. enjoys

SKILLS ACTIVITY 4: COMPOUND SUBJECTS, p. 262

1. were
2. sings
3. help
4. want
5. play
6. are
7. acts
8. support
9. is
10. were

SKILLS ACTIVITY 5: INDEFINITE PRONOUNS, p. 263

1. has
2. was
3. seems
4. jog
5. try
6. is
7. shows
8. is
9. say
10. seems

SKILLS ACTIVITY 6: *here/there*, p. 264

1. are
2. were
3. is
4. are
5. are
6. are
7. are
8. lie
9. are
10. go

SKILLS ACTIVITY 7: AMOUNT, p. 264

1. is
2. dislike
3. was
4. were
5. are
6. is
7. go
8. jog
9. is
10. is

SKILLS ACTIVITY 8: *do/does; don't/doesn't*; pp. 265–266

1. don't
2. do
3. do
4. Doesn't
5. don't
6. don't
7. does
8. do
9. doesn't
10. do

SKILLS ACTIVITY 9: NEGATIVE WORDS, pp. 266–267

Answers may vary.

1. I don't go to the movies these days.
2. I didn't have luck on my fishing trip.
3. I won't give you money to throw away.
4. She doesn't want those fish.

5. He doesn't think anything is wrong with it.
6. Lupe doesn't let anyone get near her new bicycle.
7. Chung didn't tell any of us about his high grades.
8. None of the players want to lose.
9. She didn't see any of the people.
10. The new rules aren't doing anybody any good.

SKILL TEST: SUBJECT/VERB AGREEMENT, p. 267

1. need
2. take
3. loves
4. is
5. was
6. run
7. seem
8. are
9. is
10. hop
11. were
12. is
13. come
14. was
15. is
16. was
17. is

Chapter 20 Words Often Misused or Misspelled

SKILLS ACTIVITY 1: *good/well*, p. 270

1. well
2. good
3. well
4. good
5. well
6. good, well
7. good
8. well
9. good
10. well

SKILLS ACTIVITY 2: COMPARISONS, pp. 271–272

1. fanciest
2. more intelligent
3. most intelligent
4. more humorous
5. quicker
6. smallest
7. coolest
8. more serious
9. most meticulous
10. most energetic

SKILLS ACTIVITY 3: *good/bad*, p. 272

1. worst
2. best
3. better
4. better
5. best
6. better
7. best
8. worst
9. better
10. best

SKILLS ACTIVITY 4: *less/fewer*, p. 273

1. less
2. fewer
3. less
4. fewer
5. less
6. fewer
7. less
8. fewer
9. less
10. fewer

SKILLS ACTIVITY 5: *this/that; these/those*, p. 274

1. that
2. that
3. This
4. That
5. these
6. These
7. Those
8. these
9. this
10. These

SKILLS ACTIVITY 6: *them/those/these*, p. 275

1. Those
2. those
3. those
4. those
5. These
6. those
7. those
8. those
9. those
10. those

SKILLS ACTIVITY 7: *bad/badly*, p. 275

1. bad
2. bad
3. bad
4. badly
5. bad
6. badly
7. badly
8. bad
9. badly
10. bad

SKILLS ACTIVITY 8: *between/among*, p. 276

1. among
2. between
3. Between
4. between
5. among
6. among
7. among
8. between
9. between
10. among

SKILLS ACTIVITY 9: *in/into*, p. 277

1. into
2. in
3. into
4. into
5. in
6. into
7. in
8. into
9. into
10. into

SKILLS ACTIVITY 10: *of/at*, pp. 277–278

1. where I am
2. off
3. are
4. held
5. off
6. it is
7. off
8. are
9. off
10. treasure

SKILLS ACTIVITY 11: *beside/besides*, p. 278

1. beside
2. beside
3. beside
4. Besides
5. Besides
6. beside
7. Besides
8. Besides
9. beside
10. Besides

SKILLS ACTIVITY 12: WORDS THAT SOUND ALIKE, p. 282

1. passed
2. dessert
3. quite
4. altogether
5. principal
6. They're/their
7. break
8. capitol
9. formerly
10. its

SKILLS ACTIVITY 13: SPELLING WORDS, p. 284

Answers will vary.

SKILL TEST 1: CORRECT WORDS, p. 285

1. good
2. well
3. most capable
4. friendlier
5. worse
6. better
7. fewer
8. less
9. these
10. those
11. them
12. badly
13. bad
14. among
15. Between
16. into
17. off
18. is
19. Besides
20. beside

SKILL TEST 2: SPELLING, p. 285

1. grammar
2. appearance
3. author
4. separate
5. occurrence
6. whether
7. government
8. stationery
9. privileges
10. woman
11. rhythm
12. license
13. lose
14. occasion
15. affect
16. definitions
17. principles
18. except
19. course
20. counsel

Chapter 21 Punctuation

SKILLS ACTIVITY 1: PUNCTUATING THE BEGINNINGS OF SENTENCES, p. 288

1. Why does a jet aircraft leave a "smoke" trail? It isn't smoke at all! The exhaust from a jet engine includes fuel gases and water vapor. These gases and steam hit the very cold upper air. There they form cloudlike condensation and streams of water crystals.

2. What can you do to make roller skating safe? Be sure the skate boots fit snugly and give ankle support. Wear cotton socks to help absorb perspiration. Do leg-stretching exercises for ten minutes before skating.

3, What can you do to live longer? Get lots of exercise. Active people tend to be happier and healthier than inactive people. For one thing, they stay at a sensible weight. They also recover faster from illnesses or accidents.

4. What causes volcanoes? These eruptions occur when pressures build up in underground reservoirs of molten rock and gas. The materials force their way through cracks in the earth's crust. Some volcanoes also spew ash from their surface craters. The eruption continues as long as there is great pressure underground.

SKILLS ACTIVITY 2: USING COMMAS IN A SERIES, p. 289

1. Running, walking, and swimming are excellent exercise activities.

2. Macrame, needlepoint, and knitting have become popular crafts.

3. To work, to learn, and to achieve are guideposts for many who wish to be happy.

4. Learning to read, write, and add are basic skills for success in our society.

5. To fish well you have to learn to bait a hook, you must know how to cast a line, and you must have a lot of patience.

6. Jack stuck in his thumb, he pulled out a plum, and he said he was a good boy.

7. *Cats*, *Les Miserables*, and *Phantom of the Opera* were successful Broadway musicals.

8. Dracula, Frankenstein, and Superman are fantastic literary characters with unusual powers.

9. Baking the chicken, mashing the potatoes, and cooking the peas need to be done before we can eat.

10. I opened the letter, I read it carefully, and I tore it up in disgust.

SKILLS ACTIVITY 3: USING COMMAS IN COMPOUND SENTENCES, p. 290

1. We must try to save the whales, or they will become extinct.
2. I do not like loud noise, nor do I like messy rooms.
3. Andy and Han went to lunch, and they enjoyed the food.
4. Kendra does not like to eat meat, nor does she care for junk food.
5. I would love to play the mandolin, but I have no musical talent.
6. Katrina said she would be here at seven o'clock, or she would call us.
7. Manuel loves to travel, but he has little money.
8. You are a good friend, but you annoy me sometimes.
9. There was no milk in the refrigerator, nor was there any yogurt.
10. You may want to take algebra, or you might enjoy history.

SKILLS ACTIVITY 4: COMMAS WITH INTRODUCTORY CLAUSES, PHRASES, AND WORDS, p. 291

1. After the movie, why don't you come to my house?
2. When you write me a letter, it makes me very happy.
3. No, Anthony may not leave the room.
4. Next to the table, there is a chair.
5. Well, what do you have to say for yourself?
6. While you were away, the daffodils bloomed.
7. Off to the north, high in the sky, dark clouds were forming.
8. Really, I don't know how to thank you!
9. Since Holly insists upon playing soccer, Joanna will have to play too.
10. During the summer, Dale injured his foot.

SKILLS ACTIVITY 5: COMMAS WITH PARTICIPIAL PHRASES, p. 292

1. Tormented by flies, the swimmers left the beach.
2. Dolores, enchanted by the music, smiled and sighed.
3. Attacking the problem, Mario and Francesca soon solved it.
4. Dashing out of the house, Tom forgot his lunch.
5. The girl playing the guitar is my sister.
6. Shouting with joy, Akira showed his mother the fish he had caught.
7. Julian, laughing at the joke, almost fell off his chair.
8. The girl sitting next to Leo seems to like him.
9. The woman painting the fence seems bored with her work.
10. The cat, purring with pleasure, ate its food.

SKILLS ACTIVITY 6: COMMAS WITH TRANSITIONAL WORDS AND PHRASES, p. 293

The first sentences in 1–3 and 5–10 do not need to be corrected.

1. Furthermore, I think he is jealous.
2. Nevertheless, I'll go with you tonight.
3. Therefore, you are no friend of mine.
4. The candidate, in my opinion, does not think straight.
5. On the contrary, I think she is lovely.
6. To tell the truth, I don't know the difference between them.
7. You are, of course, coming with us.
8. Some, for example, plant vegetables in community garden plots.
9. In fact, I haven't read a novel for three months.
10. Peas, for instance, grow quickly.

SKILLS ACTIVITY 7: COMMAS WITH INTERRUPTERS, p. 294

1. This group of athletes, I think, is the best team we have had.
2. Henry James, a famous novelist, wrote about high society in England.
3. Harris was, nevertheless, the winner.
4. Get in your seats, Melissa and David, and buckle your seat belts.
5. I want to visit my aunt, Ella Sanchez, before next July.
6. The result of the election, consequently, was in her favor.

7. Florence Griffith-Joyner, the Olympic champion, will go down in history as one of the greatest athletes.
8. Alonzo, do you have my bicycle?
9. Give Jim, the fellow in the yellow shirt, another sandwich.
10. Fried ice cream, an unusual dessert, is found on some menus.

SKILLS ACTIVITY 8: COMMAS IN DATES AND ADDRESSES, p. 296

1. Ella went to Houston on June 15, 1989.
2. Did you know that January 8, 1990, was the day we bought our new car?
3. October 31, 1978, was the first Halloween I can remember.
4. My graduation day was June 16, 1984.
5. On April 9, 1998, I will be twenty-one.
6. You can write to Tia Rosa at 742 Vine Street, Houston, Texas 77092-8668.
7. Juan can be reached at Box 846, Chicago, Illinois 60602-0846.
8. If you want to reach me, I'll be staying at 1400 Page Mill Road, Palo Alto, California.
9. Amos Jones lives on his farm at Rural Route 2, St. Paul, Minnesota 55182-9184.
10. Williams Drive, Ramsey, New Jersey 17466-1324 is the address of my brother.

SKILLS ACTIVITY 9: USING SEMICOLONS, COLONS, DASHES, AND PARENTHESES, p. 298

1. Amanda likes chocolate brownies and cinnamon rolls; Tony likes apple pie and peanut-butter cookies.
2. The letter said, Dear Mr. Hargrove: You can expect to receive from us next week the following items: a set of encyclopedias, two training manuals, and a contract.
3. They wanted to go—never mind that they weren't invited.
4. Along the way, we saw The Delta Queen (a luxury steamboat), five sailboats (evidently racing), and two houseboats (each being pulled by a tug).
5. When the clock showed 8:45 sharp, Monica called in her contest entry to the radio station.
6. Deep in his heart, he felt sorry for Tori; however, he knew he'd better not tell her so.

7. I'll call when I get home—oh, I just remembered: I won't be home until after midnight.
8. Some things, such as old heartaches, are best forgotten about.
9. The qualities necessary for succeeding in anything are as follows: a positive attitude, determination, and high self-esteem.
10. I am interested in numerous hobbies: stamp collecting, singing, roller skating, racquetball, and dancing—to name just a few.

SKILL TEST: PUNCTUATION, p. 299

1. Alonzo, do you have my bicycle?
2. I really enjoy Mr. Ortiz, the debate coach.
3. Throughout the bitter winter, we tried to keep warm.
4. Gosh, was I embarrassed!
5. If Natasha wants to come to the party, she is certainly welcome.
6. On July 20, 1982, Harry went to camp for the first time.
7. Yes, I promise to call Juan tonight.
8. Because the sun was so hot, the tomato plants wilted.
9. I want you to move the bed, and then I want you to paint the room.
10. Aunt Harriet ran into the room, grabbed the cage, and took our parakeet to the vet.
11. There won't, of course, be enough blankets to keep everyone warm.
12. You must study the following verbs: *ride*, *burst*, *catch*, and *drink*.
13. Is there a way to make amends? Unfortunately, I don't think so.
14. A valentine, such as the ones they used to send at the turn of the century, can easily be made by hand.
15. Anthony, I need some help quick!
16. Mark Twain, the wonderful humorist, gave us many memorable sayings.
17. August 14 was marked as the day for the rally; however, it rained too hard to hold it.
18. Why do they keep changing prime-time shows on TV?
19. I know I should eat liver, parsley, and spinach, but I hate all three of these foods.
20. Please, Maria, stop acting so sulky, and—before you know it—you'll feel happy again.

Chapter 22 Using Apostrophes and Quotations

SKILLS ACTIVITY 1: SINGULAR AND PLURAL POSSESSIVES, p. 302

1. city's
2. cities'
3. Morris's
4. mice's
5. chief's
6. phone's
7. hero's
8. Ms. Willis's
9. child's
10. children's

SKILLS ACTIVITY 2: PLACING APOSTROPHES CORRECTLY, p. 303

1. a baby's cry
2. a dollar's worth
3. women's shoe sizes
4. the city's taxes
5. a woman's shoe size
6. a knife's blade
7. all the knives' blades
8. one radio's speakers
9. several speakers' volume
10. last evening's newscasts

SKILLS ACTIVITY 3: SHOWING POSSESSION, p. 303

1. Kansas City's team
2. the men's clothing store
3. a woman's beauty
4. New Orleans's French Quarter
5. Ms. Wallace's car
6. the children's programs
7. the personnel director's forms
8. ancient Greece's dramas
9. the club members' rules
10. the actress's costumes

SKILLS ACTIVITY 4: FORMING CONTRACTIONS, p. 304

1. she'll
2. he's
3. haven't
4. don't
5. you're
6. I'm
7. can't
8. doesn't
9. I've
10. they're

SKILLS ACTIVITY 5: ADDING CONTRACTIONS, p. 304

1. You've seen what's in style for the coming season.
2. Shouldn't that stereo volume be turned down?
3. It's my opinion that you weren't on the right track.
4. Weren't those committee meetings much too long?
5. They've found that Chicago isn't as windy as many other cities.
6. You'll find that girls and boys won't agree on what to play.
7. Don't assume that what hasn't worked can't eventually work.
8. We've heard your excuses, and they don't make any sense.
9. That doesn't mean you couldn't hit on some bright ideas.
10. I hope you're telling me the truth when you say she'll be here soon.

SKILLS ACTIVITY 6: PUNCTUATING QUOTATIONS, p. 306

1. The steward said, "Please have your boarding passes ready."
2. The sign said, "This way out."
3. "The fall semester begins after Labor Day," said the announcement.
4. "Why can't vacations last longer?" complained the tourists.
5. The sign flashed, "Don't walk."
6. The weather report warned, "Cloudy with a chance of rain."
7. "What a terrible show," shouted the TV viewers.
8. "Give me a roast beef on rye," said the customer.
9. "Do you want to sit in the non-smoking section?" asked the ticket agent.
10. "How high can prices get?" exclaimed the shopper.

SKILLS ACTIVITY 7: CREATING DIRECT QUOTATIONS, p. 306

1. The operator said, "The number has been changed."
2. The pilot suggested, "Keep your seatbelts fastened."
3. The weather service repeated, "The tornado warnings have been cancelled."
4. The paper said, "The transit fare will go up again."
5. The TV announcer repeated, "We are having operating difficulties."
6. The customer asked, "Where are the best seats?"

7. The answering machine said, "Give your message at the beep sound."
8. The ad shouted, "Buy America's favorite cleanser."
9. The clerk explained, "A computer breakdown lost the order."
10. The woman asked, "When can I see a replay of the special events tape?"

SKILLS ACTIVITY 8: PUNCTUATING DIALOGUE, p. 307

1. "What are you going to pay me for this work?" asked Milt.
   "I'll pay you what you're worth," replied his boss.
   "I'd rather have some money," said Milt.
2. The guest said, "I want to leave a 6:00 call."
   "We're all out of 6:00 calls," replied the hotel clerk.
   "The call me twice at 3:00!" exclaimed the guest.
3. "I've lost my wallet," shouted Max.
   "Where did you lose it?" asked Gilda.
   "Over there," replied Max.
   "They why are you looking for it over here?" asked Gilda.
   "There's more light over here!" explained Max.

SKILLS ACTIVITY 9: WRITING DIALOGUE, p. 307

Answers will vary.

SKILL TEST: APOSTROPHES AND QUOTATIONS, pp. 307–308

1. Some of the world's fastest trains aren't in the United States, but in Japan and France.
2. Dallas's huge airport is one of Texas's great showplaces, according to the promotional brochure.
3. Wasn't *Hello Dolly* based on Thornton Wilder's *The Matchmaker*?
4. She'll come when she's good and ready.
5. Some women's organizations have changed many people's way of thinking.
6. They say that one person's meat is another's poison.

7. "One person's meat is another's poison," my aunt Ida used to say to her brothers when they argued politics.
8. That movie's ending can't be as good as its beginning.
9. Aren't the children's programs shown on Saturday morning?
10. Everyone's hope was to get the star's autograph.
11. Maurice yelled "Thief! Thief!" even though the man hadn't yet tried to steal anything.
12. You'll find that a fool's money is foolishly spent.
13. "A fool's money is foolishly spent!" Judy exclaimed when Tony's sister asked her to buy some raffle tickets.
14. Why can't everyone's favorite program be on at the right time?
15. It's a shame that Martin's watch hasn't worked right since he bought it.
16. Shouldn't the new car's mileage be better than the old?
17. The sign said "This way out," but they didn't pay attention and got lost.
18. Atlanta's rapid transit system isn't the country's largest, but it's the newest.
19. Candice's best idea wasn't even heard before the group's president adjourned the meeting.
20. When we entered the theatre the usher said, "The play's already started. You'll have to wait until intermission to be seated."

Chapter 23 Capitalization and Abbreviation

SKILLS ACTIVITY 1: CAPITALIZING PROPER NOUNS, p. 310

1. Many companies have kept their family name, such as the Pillsbury Company.
2. The Atlantic Ocean can be treacherously stormy.
3. Where is the campus of Florida State University?
4. The Eiffel Tower was once the tallest structure in the world.
5. One of our most picturesque cities is San Antonio.
6. For some reason, Chinese cooking is becoming more popular.
7. One holiday that occurs in the fall is Columbus Day.
8. I have always wanted to attend a World Series game.
9. You must be familiar with many of the English writers of the Renaissance.
10. The Battle of the Coral Sea occurred during stormy weather.

SKILLS ACTIVITY 2: COMMON NOUNS AND PROPER NOUNS, p. 311

Answers will vary.

SKILLS ACTIVITY 3: CAPITALIZING TITLES, p. 312

1. James Jones's <u>From Here to Eternity</u> is another World War II novel.
2. "Once by the Pacific" is a poem by Robert Frost.
3. The James Dean movie, <u>Rebel without a Cause,</u> is a classic.
4. Robert Louis Stevenson's "A Lodging for the Night" is a good short story.
5. <u>Road and Track</u> is a favorite magazine for car buffs.
6. The chapter, "Food for Thought," tells how to eat wisely.
7. <u>Wind, Sand, and Stars</u> is an unusual book about the early days of flying.
8. The <u>Atlanta Constitution</u> is an influential newspaper in the South.

9. Songs like "Body and Soul" never seem out of date.
10. T. S. Eliot's "The Waste Land" is a famous modern poem.

SKILLS ACTIVITY 4: PUNCTUATING TITLES, p. 313

1. The novel, <u>Tender is the Night,</u> is one of Fitzgerald's best.
2. Emily Dickinson's poem, "I Never Saw a Moor," is probably her most famous.
3. One of the great TV successes is the show "Sesame Street."
4. The <u>Washington Post</u> has outstanding reporting.
5. Poe's "The Tell-Tale Heart" is a chilling short story.
6. A movie like <u>Raiders of the Lost Ark</u> is shown again and again.
7. "I Got Rhythm" is a favorite old song.
8. Read the article, "How Cigarettes Kill."
9. The novel, <u>All the King's Men,</u> is about politics.
10. The short story, "The Cask of Amontillado," is Poe at his best.

SKILLS ACTIVITY 5: PUNCTUATING AND CAPITALIZING NAMES, p. 314

1. Both dentists, Dr. J. L. Brace and Dr. Kathleen D. Bridges, attended.
2. Mayor Alvarez asked for more city funds from Gov. Dahler.
3. Mrs. Harris goes to the hair stylist, Mr. Stiles.
4. Bruce Katz works part time at the animal hospital for Dr. Setter.
5. Two Washington regulars are Sen. Willis Quick and Rep. J. B. Nimble.
6. It didn't take long for Mr. Gil T. Persons to call his lawyer, Ms. I. M. Lawless.
7. The new tennis stars are Jane Court and Buddy Racket.
8. Prof. H. V. Braines and Prof. O. B. Smart are coauthors of a textbook.
9. Did Sen. M. T. Tung or Rep. Constance Noyes speak at the rally?
10. On exhibit were paintings by Ms. Dabble and Mr. Brush.

SKILLS ACTIVITY 6: USING STANDARD ABBREVIATIONS, p. 316

1. lb.
2. C
3. CO
4. CT
5. AR
6. AZ

7. ME
8. MD
9. MA
10. FM
11. qt.
12. mi.
13. km
14. cm
15. kg
16. l

SKILLS ACTIVITY 7: WRITING CORRECT ABBREVIATIONS, pp. 316–317

1. First-run movies are at 9:00 P.M. on HBO.
2. It is 2190 km, or 1111 mi., between Dallas and Miami.
3. Many of the NATO nations are also in the EEC.
4. In the eastern time zone, 8:00 to 11:00 P.M. is TV prime time.
5. Does the recipe call for a tsp. or a tbsp. of curry powder?
6. I learned that 60 mi. is nearly the same as 100 km.
7. Was Hallmark or IBM the sponsor of the holiday special on CBS?
8. The stakeout was at a Ninth Ave. address on Sept. 12.
9. A body temperature of 37°C is normal, while 38°C is feverish.
10. Soft drinks are sold by the l, but the qt. is still the usual size for milk.

SKILLS ACTIVITY 8: WRITING ADDRESSES CORRECTLY, pp. 317–318

1. 11530 Milam Avenue
   Houston, TX 77090-2449
2. 5220 Valley Blvd.
   Phoenix, AZ 85033-6487
3. 72 Palisade Terr.
   San Diego, CA 92117-1179
4. 4950 Ringling Drive
   Sarasota, FL 33582-4894
5. 7825 Lee Avenue
   Atlanta, GA 30312-4520
6. 3915 Boulder Ave.
   Denver, CO 80211-9131
7. 5935 Oakland Pkwy.
   Houston, TX 75231-0055
8. 3550 Country Club Lane
   Kansas City, MO 64112-2416
9. 6212 Riverview Blvd.
   Alexandria, VA 22317-2301
10. 33 Ogden Avenue
    Hindsdale, IL 60521-6989

SKILLS ACTIVITY 9: WRITING DATES CORRECTLY, p. 319

1. The next Kentucky Derby will take place on Saturday, May 4, 1998.
2. Our nation's birthday is July 4, 1776.
3. June 6, 1944, was the beginning of the greatest military invasion in history.
4. Jan. 8 is my brother's birthday.
5. The date on the letter, 8/14/95, was not clearly written.
6. On February 25, 1924, Montuda became a citizen of the United States.
7. I believe that particular event took place in April 1978.
8. When Tues., September 5 arrives, we'll be in New York City.
9. Their wedding is set for Sunday, June 18, 1998.
10. Dates such as November 27, 1960, and December 23, 1957, stick in my mind.

SKILL TEST: USING CAPITALS AND ABBREVIATIONS, p. 319

1. Aunt Cynthia wrote a letter to Ms. Alvarez on my behalf.
2. "The Outcasts of Poker Flat" by Bret Harte was a good story.
3. She plans to attend Washington State University in September 1998.
4. The population of New Jersey is about the same as that of Japan.
5. The Senator wanted to see Dr. Molnar right away.
6. Does PBS get any funding from the general public?
7. There is both a Portland, ME, and a Portland, OR.
8. Don't drive over 65 mph. on the Jefferson Freeway.
9. Do you like Italian or French dressing on your salad?
10. Before you know it, Monday, September 5 will be here.
11. The library doesn't subscribe to <u>Reader's Digest</u> any longer.
12. Have you read that great article "How to Make a Fortune in the Stock Market"?
13. They called Mrs. Helen K. Russell to the stand.
14. Which is the world's longest river, the Nile or the Amazon?
15. They took an apartment at 516 Riverside Drive in Manhattan.
16. The songwriter, Jerome Kern, wrote "Smoke Gets in Your Eyes."
17. Let's go to the Orpheum Theater and see <u>M.A.S.H.</u>
18. Is this the week for the Superbowl or the World Series?

19. Prof. Thomas Schuller lectured at the annual May Day program.

20. Neither Los Angeles nor San Francisco is the capital of California.

Selected Bibliography

Barkas, J. L. *How to Write Like a Professional*. New York: Arco Publishing, 1985.
Excellent tips on the realities and challenges of professional writing. Good for students and teachers.

Berthoff, Ann E. *Forming/Thinking/Writing: The Composing Imagination*. Montclair, NJ: Boynton/Cook, 1982.
This book investigates the composing process. "The Making of Meaning," "A Method of Composing," and "Construing and Constructing" are the three major sections of the text. Models and exercises help to clarify the instruction.

Horton, Susan. *Thinking Through Writing*. Baltimore: Johns Hopkins University Press, 1982.

Hughes, Elaine. *Writing from the Inner Self*. New York: HarperCollins College Publishers, 1994.
A collection of writing and meditation exercises designed to free creativity and inspire imagination. Developed and tested in the classroom.

Kirby, Dan, and Tom Liner. *Inside Out: Developmental Strategies for Teaching Writing*. Montclair, NJ: Boynton/Cook, 1981.
This is a practical book that contains a wealth of activities and teaching strategies.

Macrorie, Ken. *Searching Writing*. Rochelle Park, NJ: Hayden Book Co., 1980.

———. *Telling Writing*. Rochelle Park, NJ: Hayden Book Co., 1980.

———. *Writing to Be Read*. Rochelle Park, NJ: Hayden Book Co., 1976.

———. *A Vulnerable Teacher*. Rochelle Park, NJ: Hayden Book Co., 1974.

———. *Uptaught*. Rochelle Park, NJ: Hayden Book Co., 1970.
Emphasizing personal feelings and experiences as foundations for growth in writing, Macrorie presents a convincing case for his philosophy of teaching writing.

Miller, James, and Elizabeth Morse-Cluley. *How to Write Book Reports*. New York: Arco Publishing, 1984.
An excellent book on a limited but important subject for many teachers.

Moffett, James. *Coming on Center*. Montclair, NJ: Boynton/Cook, 1982.

———. *Active Voice*. Montclair, NJ: Boynton/Cook, 1982.

———, and Betty J. Wagner. *Student-Centered Language Arts and Reading, K–13*. Boston: Houghton, Mifflin, 1976.
Coming on Center is a collection of articles by Moffett on teaching language arts. *Active Voice* summarizes his writing program. *Student-Centered Language Arts and Reading, K–13* is a detailed book about his thinking on teaching a total language arts program. The three books comprise a fascinating and valuable panorama of immensely rewarding insights into how language works and how it can be taught by one of the keenest minds in the modern educational world.

Mulkerne, Donald J., Jr. *Perfect Term Paper: Step-by-Step.* New York: Anchor Books, 1988.
A practical approach to the writing of term papers.

Ponsot, Marie, and Rosemary Deen. *Beat Not the Poor Desk: Writing: What To Teach, How To Teach It, and Why.* Montclair, NJ: Boynton/Cook, 1982.
An approach to teaching writing inductively, this book should provide a variety of new ideas for the classroom teacher.

Rico, Gabriele. *Writing the Natural Way: Using Right-Brain Techniques to Release Your Expressive Powers.* New York: St. Martin's Press, 1983.
Combines "right-brain" research with innovative teaching techniques such as clustering to tap the inner resources of brainpower for writing. A fascinating and useful book that is a product of classroom testing.

Sebranek, Patrick, and Dave Kemper. *The Write Source.* Box J, Burlington, WI 53108.
A terrific handbook and teaching resource for teachers and students on all aspects of writing, including grammar.

Silverman, Jay, Elaine Hughes, and Diana Roberts Wienbroer. *Rules of Thumb: A Guide for Writers.* 3d ed. New York: McGraw-Hill, Inc., 1996.
An excellent brief and easy-to-use handbook that covers the essentials of correct usage.

Strunk, William, Jr., and E. B. White. *The Elements of Style.* 3d ed. New York: Macmillan, 1979.
A classic in the field, it still is worth reading more than once.